ROMANCE OF MEMORIES

BROKEN PROMISE

SHUBHAM SINGH

Copyright © Shubham Singh
All Rights Reserved.

ISBN 979-888569522-0

Contents

Contents

Acknowledgements

I am deeply thankful to Saakshi Sharma for her loving support and vital part in transforming the manuscript with this book and bringing it out into the world.

Finally, I would like to express my love and gratitude to my mother and father, without whom this book would not have come into existence, and to the greatest guru of all: *Life*

About The Author

The author, Shubham Singh, comes from Purnea - a beautiful place in Bihar. He's currently pursuing his law degree, which is among one of his many dreams. He believes in gaining knowledge and precise work as much as it is possible.

His approximation of success is that "keep working on yourself and things around you" this is the definition of true success when you achieve what you want to. He believes

"Life is a journey of thousand steps, on few you will tumble and few will pass with joy"

He loves to write, and portray what he see's through his eyes. He expresses his emotion, pain and gratitude with war through his pen.

"He says, his pen whispers to him in his dream and narrates the unheard, throughout the mist and cloud in darkness with spark in her eyes."

From time to time he has tried to display his love of writing through his creation, and he loves doing it.

Introduction

Romance of Memories opens an insight to the beauty of vibes that a person goes through the hymn of love, the feeling, the tears, pain, and pleasure of missing and dreaming for someone who has been unknown is such a complex element of love that it grows day by day and we nourish it like a child. The trigonometry between heart, brain, and breath changes dramatically and nothing remains under our control.

It sounds so sweet to everyone that love is like the first rain of the monsoon but the marks it leaves on the soul is undescribable. One can describe love in the most fascinating way he or she can but the true question remains in silence that, What is love?, Is love beautiful or the feeling of loving someone unconditionally is beautiful? Which is more true being with love or always staying in sence that one day love will be mine? the question is debatable and everyone has their own answer to this question.

Romance of Memories tries to answer these questions in a poetic way trying to cover the essence of love in a dramatic twist, revealing the true nature of love in all forms.

The book name Romance of Memories will ensure that the reader goes through a journey of emotion which will reflect somewhere their soul and rollercoaster them through their past or help them recall the unword moment that might have lost on the pillow at night.

The Poet through his belive in his writing and the way he jumbles the words have tried to picture events of a lonely lover in the woods wondering, singing, and admiring his beloved.

"Love is for centuries, is for ages" is what poets belives but my friends the poet of this book believe that love fades and life needs a new start.

Someone once told the Poet that "His love is seasonal, it changes to time", poet's heart was shattered into pieces like stars at night. He learned from life that love isn't permanent it is like leaf of a tree, will fall (fail) one day and a new one will come with the first air of spring.

1. In The Light Of Moon

I wishpered to the silence
Is it scary ?
Are you afraid of Dark?
Why don't you smile?
Aren't, you in love?
with Fear of breathe
The cold is taking over,
And I smell the touch,
On my veins,
In The Light Of Moon!
I wonder, if you will answer
It is scary!
In The Light Of Moon.

2. Night

Light Scares to-,
fall on your breath
My heartbeat is unregular
It stops when I see
your pale lips,
Pain is taking over my lungs
Spreading to my heart
Oh! Night
Can I cry?
Promise me, no one will know?
My tears will fall,
But you will hide.
On her Dry lips.

3. Dry Lips

My tears fall,
On her dry lips,
went inside.
Oh! Wind
Will it give her life?
When my pain through,
My tears get into her heart,
Will her dry lips, joy?
If it?
I would cry my heart,
My love, My Sorrow,
Melting in the warmth of my eyes.
On her Dry Lips!

4. Smile

I Smile?

Did I?

or it's just another phase,

of my love dying in my arms?

Recalling moments in her last breath

All seems, true-alive

Hello my love

Am I Smiling?

or it's just our moment,

Let's fall in love!

5. Rusting

It begins with
Cloud forming over our head
The mist in the air turned dust
My memory? Rusting!
It is Funny!
How things are getting muddy,
before it could rain.
The surface is dry, rough
My fingers feel numb,
So do my love in my memory.

6. Melting

The Shadow is melting
In the light
Is it spring?
Butterfly, flies
Here sits one on her lips,
Tries to get in,
But couldn't - her teeth
Is it time to say "GOOD BYE",
To my Love?
And Smell her Hairs for last time.
I Know, She will melt,
Decay! On Rose bed,
Under the soil for ages!

7. Life

It's been ages,
I saw you,
Holded your hand,
Now alone in this-alien land,
The wind blew strange,
Shadow is unknown,
How lonely?
Can it be without your touch,
It doesn't even reflect "My Life".

8. Silence

Love, my words aren't-
Silent! They are dipped in honey
Clock ar ticking, Time?
Love, Why you smile?
It isn't Funny!
I can smell, fishy
Silence, Mourn-Morn,
I know time has come.
And things will fade,
But you will remain
As Silence in my Heart!

9. Promise

Love, Is it true,
things Changes, Time
Changes?
Will you?
Promise me, eternity
In your arms, without
a breath of qualm.
Promise to quench,
your lust with my youth.
And Promise, to smile,
When I Die.

10. Addictive

Am I in deep sleep?
My eyes are unclosed,
Can see your hands,
Hear your smell in woods
Wish to follow, your voice
But couldn't, My-legs
Feels life-less,
Are you buried?
Why, things are blurred?
Your Smell isn't addictive?
Am I alive?
It feels heavy on my chest,
Are you Buried over me?
My Love, Talk to me?
Your silence, Isn't lovable,
It is Scary!

11. Light

When I spell, Love
It's Light in my Life,
Darkness has gone,
And I smile.
Springtime? You So bright,
Am I in love?
goose-bumps
It isn't Raining!
Still, I see Rainbow, and
it shines!

12. Envelope

My Mistress, Handed
Envelope Of Love,
Written in melancholy,
Dip in her tears,
fell like pearls, on
white sheet.
Letter Ends in Question,
Do I still love her?
Is She young?
Does her smell attract my senses?
I wrote with Smile,
Her lust is only thing,
that I wish to breathe, through
my senses!

13. Is It Love?

When my eyes are closed,
And you smoke to my ears,
sweat through my neck, freeze
I hear you, laugh-giggle
in dark,
The air is excited,
Playing naughty,
I see a hand, and
a light, taking me away
in dream,
Hear a whisper,
Echoing, Is it love?
Is It Love?

14. Morn

It is raining, birds chirping
Leafs are wet,
and my ears on my mistress's heart,
It is mysterious, magical
pleasing, listening to her breath,
Her warmth, feels as
I reborn,
In Morn of Love!

15. Essence of Love

Many of times
It feels like,
Love has faded,
Has fallen in darkness,
Where is daylight,
To spark,
The seed of trust,
The essence of magic,
The bond of blood,
Heaven need to be built,
From ashes of dead,
In the valley of melancholy,
It needs to be born,
The seed of love,
For rainbow, &
Sunlight!

16. Butterfly

Leaf has fallen,
Yellow & Pale
Spring, Does it Smell?
See how butterfly,
rhyme the melody,
Beautiful and Smooth.
Like Infinity, Like Zero,
inspires to be air in bubble,
with new life,
new song & Melody

17. Coldness

It shattered my hope,
Buried my sole,
When I learned
I lost you when I found you
The cold wind froze my breath,
It felt as I was on voyage in Antarctica
With broken oars, direction-less
traveling through memory,
Recalling the coldness of trust
That you broke!

18. Love

I watched myself becoming
Puppet of your command,
Smiling, Gasping the terror of love
Romancing through your blonde hairs,
Climbing to your lips,
Whispering, I trust you, my love
Walking on double edge sword

19. Chock

My heart aches silently,
drowning, breathing
Poison in air,
Love, It chock
Can I whiff fresh air?
She smiled, and hugged me
Saying breath me love,
I stayed Chocking,
until my heart died in her arms.

20. Fascinate

Now cloud don't fascinate,
Melody has no rhyme,
Song that I used to sing, has died
Now light is dipped in dark, blurred
Sadness has surrounded my heart
Through veins is reaching my lungs,
brain & Stomach.
It feels pain, terror
As me sitting in darkness,
where my eyes play another song.

21. My Strength

I lost my health
In year bubble
But remains my wealth
By my side,
My weakness,
My strength,
My lover unconditionally
Without prejudice my interest
And without changing my vision
I look the world.

22. Mistress

Hypnotize my brain,
My heart, my breath
My soul to love
Love you like a rose,
Asking angel
The alien of foreign land
How is my mistress?
Lovable? Adorable?
God bless me infinity in her arms

23. Darkness

Darkness is all I heard,
The day you whispered "love"
My destiny, my desire
To love, the lost
I tried
I broke
I breathe on mirror,
But couldn't see my breath,
Darkness, my eyes blind
Covered with love
Truth or lie
Sunset or shine
Darkness is all I heard.

24. My Love

Listening to echo
In the woods
Ran toward unknown,
With heavy heart, missing
Felt vacuum of thought
Closed eyes, felt your hand,
Holding it,
I wish I could discover
New land of love & surprises
Beyond the poles ever foot by men

25. Memories

Is it hard to believe,
Your skin is still on my lips,
Smell, on my bed,
Tingling into my hair,
Kisses on my neck,
Love me back my memories,
Love me back,
In the bubble of us,
Useless to world.